Portage Township Schools
ESL Program

Introducción a los padres

We Both Read es la primera serie de libros diseñada para invitar a padres e hijos a compartir la lectura de un cuento, por turnos y en voz alta. Esta "lectura compartida" —que se ha desarrollado en conjunto con especialistas en primeras lecturas— invita a los padres a leer los textos más complejos en la página de la izquierda. Luego, les toca a los niños leer las páginas de la derecha, que contienen textos más sencillos, escritos específicamente para primeros lectores.

Leer en voz alta es una de las actividades más importantes que los padres comparten con sus hijos para ayudarlos a desarrollar la lectura. Sin embargo, *We Both Read* no es solo leerle *a* un niño, sino que les permite a los padres leer *con* el niño. *We Both Read* es más poderoso y efectivo porque combina dos elementos claves del aprendizaje: "demostración" (el padre lee) y "aplicación" (el niño lee). El resultado no es solo que el niño aprende a leer más rápido, ¡sino que ambos disfrutan y se enriquecen con esta experiencia!

Sería más útil si usted lee el libro completo y en voz alta la primera vez, y luego invita a su niño a participar en una segunda lectura. En algunos libros, las palabras más difíciles se presentan por primera vez en **negritas** en el texto del padre. Señalar o conversar sobre estas palabras ayudará a su niño a familiarizarse con estas y a ampliar su vocabulario. También notará que el ícono "lee el padre" ⌒ precede el texto del padre y el ícono de "lee el niño" ⌒ precede el texto del niño.

Lo invitamos a compartir y a relacionarse con su niño mientras leen el libro juntos. Si su hijo tiene dificultad, usted puede mencionar algunas cosas que lo ayuden. "Decir cada sonido" es bueno, pero puede que esto no funcione con todas las palabras. Los niños pueden hallar pistas en las palabras del cuento, en el contexto de las oraciones e incluso de las imágenes. Algunos cuentos incluyen patrones y rimas que los ayudarán. También le podría ser útil a su niño tocar las palabras con su dedo mientras leen para conectar mejor el sonido de la voz con la palabra impresa.

¡Al compartir los libros de *We Both Read*, usted y su hijo vivirán juntos la fascinante aventura de la lectura! Es una manera divertida y fácil de animar y ayudar a su niño a leer —¡y una maravillosa manera de preparar a su niño para disfrutar de la lectura durante toda su vida!

Parent's Introduction

We Both Read is the first series of books designed to invite parents and children to share the reading of a story by taking turns reading aloud. This "shared reading" innovation, which was developed with reading education specialists, invites parents to read the more complex text and storyline on the left-hand pages. Children are encouraged to read the right-hand pages, which feature less complex text and storyline, specifically written for the beginning reader.

Reading aloud is one of the most important activities parents can share with their child to assist in his or her reading development. However, *We Both Read* goes beyond reading *to* a child and allows parents to share the reading *with* a child. *We Both Read* is so powerful and effective because it combines two key elements in learning: "modeling" (the parent reads) and "doing" (the child reads). The result is not only faster reading development for the child, but a much more enjoyable and enriching experience for both!

You may find it helpful to read the entire book aloud yourself the first time, then invite your child to participate in the second reading. In some books, a few more difficult words will first be introduced in the parent's text, distinguished with **bold lettering**. Pointing out, and even discussing, these words will help familiarize your child with them and help to build your child's vocabulary. Also, note that a "talking parent" icon ⟲ precedes the parent's text and a "talking child" icon ⟲ precedes the child's text.

We encourage you to share and interact with your child as you read the book together. If your child is having difficulty, you might want to mention a few things to help him or her. "Sounding out" is good, but it will not work with all words. Children can pick up clues about the words they are reading from the story, the context of the sentence, or even the pictures. Some stories have rhyming patterns that might help. It might also help them to touch the words with their finger as they read, to better connect the voice sound and the printed word.

Sharing the *We Both Read* books together will engage you and your child in an interactive adventure in reading! It is a fun and easy way to encourage and help your child to read—and a wonderful way to start your child off on a lifetime of reading enjoyment!

We Both Read: About Space
Acerca del espacio

This revised and updated edition is dedicated with appreciation
to the past, present, and future pioneers of space.

*Esta edición actualizada está dedicada con mucho
agradecimiento a los pioneros del espacio del pasado,
a los del presente y a los del futuro.*

Text Copyright © 2008, 2001 by Treasure Bay
Translation services provided by Cambridge BrickHouse, Inc.
Spanish translation © 2010 by Treasure Bay, Inc.
All rights reserved.

Images courtesy of NASA, NSSDC, NASA/JPL-Caltech, and NASA/JSC.

We Both Read® is a registered trademark of Treasure Bay, Inc.

Published by Treasure Bay, Inc.
P.O. Box 119
Novato, CA 94948

PRINTED IN SINGAPORE

Library of Congress Catalog Card Number: 2010932685

ISBN: 978-1-60115-052-3

We Both Read® Books
Patent No. 5,957,693

Visit us online at:
www.TreasureBayBooks.com

PR 11/10

We Both Read®

About Space

Acerca del espacio

By Jana Carson

Translated by Diego Mansilla

TREASURE BAY

Let's take a journey into space, where we will see wondrous sights and make incredible discoveries.

What is space? Space is the **universe**. The **universe** contains everything!

Hagamos un viaje al espacio, donde veremos escenas maravillosas y haremos descubrimientos increíbles.

*¿Qué es el espacio? El espacio es el **universo**. ¡Y el **universo** lo contiene todo!*

Have you ever looked way up at the sky? It seems to go on forever! Yet, what we see in our sky is only a very tiny part of the **universe**.

*¿Alguna vez has mirado al cielo? Parece no tener fin. Sin embargo, lo que vemos en el cielo es solo una pequeña parte del **universo**.*

All of the galaxies, planets, stars, meteors, asteroids, and even space stations are part of the universe.

A galaxy is a large system of stars held together in a group by gravity. We live in a galaxy called the **Milky Way**. We are able to view many of the stars in our galaxy through the use of a telescope.

Todas las galaxias, los planetas, las estrellas, los meteoros, los asteroides y hasta las estaciones espaciales son parte del universo.

*Una galaxia es un gran sistema de estrellas que se mantienen juntas por acción de la gravedad. Vivimos en una galaxia llamada **Vía Láctea**. Podemos ver muchas de las estrellas de nuestra galaxia por medio de un telescopio.*

Long ago, people could only look at the stars with their eyes. The stars of the **Milky Way** looked like a white streak in the sky.

*Hace mucho tiempo, la gente solo podía usar sus ojos para ver las estrellas. Las estrellas de la **Vía Láctea** parecían una franja blanca en el cielo.*

Planets of our Solar System (relative size and position not shown)
Planetas de nuestro Sistema Solar (no se muestran sus dimensiones ni posiciones relativas)

Within a galaxy there may be many **solar systems**. A **solar system** is made up of a sun and everything that moves around it.

Our **solar system** exists within the Milky Way galaxy. It includes all the planets and their moons, as well as the comets, asteroids, and space objects that orbit, or move in circles, around the Sun.

*Dentro de una galaxia pueden haber muchos **sistemas solares**. Un **sistema solar** está formado por un sol y todo lo que se mueve a su alrededor.*

*Nuestro **sistema solar** se encuentra en la Vía Láctea. Este incluye todos los planetas y sus lunas, así como los cometas, asteroides y cuerpos celestes que orbitan, o se mueven en círculos, alrededor del Sol.*

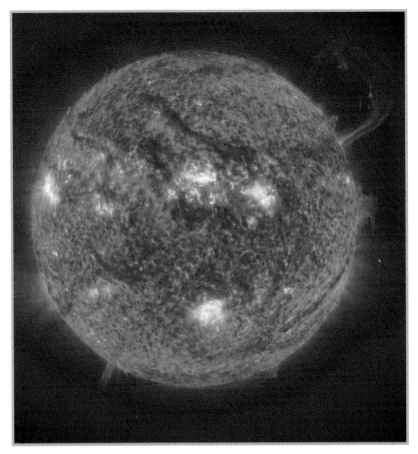

There is a sun in the center of every **solar system**. A sun is really a star. Without our Sun, there could be no life in our solar system.

*Hay un sol en el centro de cada **sistema solar**. Un sol es, en realidad, una estrella. Sin nuestro Sol, no habría vida en nuestro sistema solar.*

The planet we live on is called the Earth. Other planets in our solar system are **Mercury**, Venus, Mars, Jupiter, Saturn, Uranus, and Neptune.

Mercury is the closest planet to our Sun. The temperature on the planet's surface is hot enough to melt a metal pan!

*El planeta en que vivimos se llama Tierra. Otros planetas en nuestro sistema solar son **Mercurio**, Venus, Marte, Júpiter, Saturno, Urano y Neptuno.*

***Mercurio** es el planeta más cercano al Sol. ¡La temperatura en la superficie de ese planeta es suficiente para derretir una sartén de metal!*

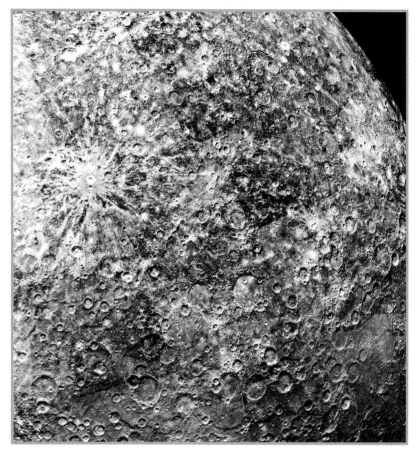

Mercury is a small planet. It is about the size of our Moon. It is very, very hot on **Mercury**. It is too hot for people to live there!

*Mercurio es un planeta pequeño. Es como del tamaño de nuestra Luna. Hace mucho, mucho calor en **Mercurio**. ¡Hace demasiado calor para vivir allí!*

Venus and Earth are similar in size and they both have mountains, valleys, and plains. But there are no oceans or life of any kind on **Venus**.

Venus is covered with thick clouds. There are always huge thunderstorms in these clouds.

Venus y la Tierra tienen tamaños similares y los dos tienen montañas, valles y llanuras. Pero no hay océanos ni ninguna clase de vida en Venus.

Venus está cubierto de nubes densas. Siempre hay grandes tormentas en estas nubes.

Venus is called the Evening Star because it looks so bright in our night sky.

*A **Venus** lo llaman el Lucero de la tarde porque brilla mucho en el cielo oscuro.*

Mars is called the red planet. **Space probes** were sent to **Mars** by the United States and other countries to collect information about the Martian soil and atmosphere. Through these experiments, it was discovered that the dirt on **Mars** contains lots of iron. The iron is what gives **Mars** its reddish color.

*A **Marte** lo llaman el planeta rojo. Los Estados Unidos y otros países enviaron **sondas espaciales** a **Marte** para obtener información acerca del suelo y la atmósfera marciana. Mediante estos experimentos se descubrió que el suelo de **Marte** contiene mucho hierro. El hierro es lo que le da a **Marte** su color rojo.*

Is there life on **Mars**? People who study space wanted to know the answer. They sent **space probes** to **Mars**. The **space probes** looked, but found no life there.

*¿Hay vida en **Marte**? La gente que estudia el espacio quería saber la respuesta. Enviaron **sondas espaciales** a **Marte**. Las **sondas espaciales** buscaron alguna forma de vida, pero no la encontraron.*

Jupiter is the largest planet in our solar system. There are terrific lightning bolts and huge gas storms in **Jupiter's** atmosphere.

A large area of swirling gas called the Great Red Spot is believed to be a hurricane-like storm.

***Júpiter** es el planeta más grande de nuestro sistema solar. Hay tremendos relámpagos y enormes tormentas de gas en la atmósfera de **Júpiter**.*

Se cree que la Gran Mancha Roja es una gran cantidad de gas que gira velozmente, creando un gigantesco huracán.

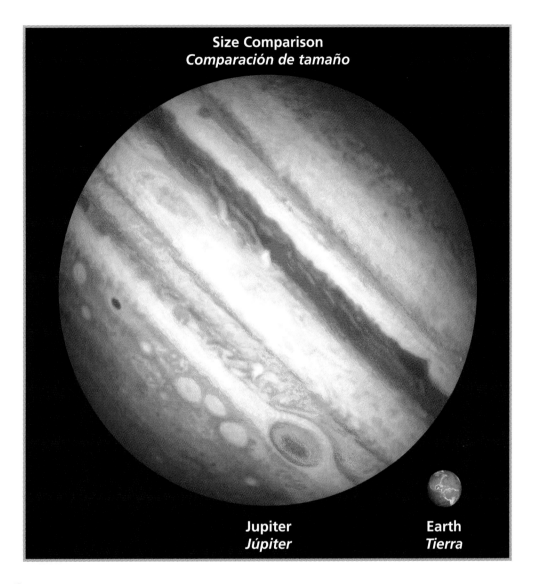

Size Comparison
Comparación de tamaño

Jupiter
Júpiter

Earth
Tierra

Jupiter is very, very big! All of the other planets in our solar system could fit inside of **Jupiter**.

*¡**Júpiter** es muy, muy grande! Todos los demás planetas del sistema solar podrían caber dentro de **Júpiter**.*

15

Saturn is a planet that spins rapidly on its axis—just like a spinning top. This rapid spinning causes something amazing to happen. The top and bottom of the planet flatten out!

It is believed that there are over 1,000 rings surrounding **Saturn**. The rings are actually particles of ice and dust.

Saturno es un planeta que gira rápidamente sobre su eje, como un trompo en movimiento. Este movimiento rápido hace que suceda algo increíble. ¡La parte superior e inferior del planeta se aplanan!

*Se cree que hay más de 1000 anillos alrededor de **Saturno**. Los anillos son, en realidad, partículas de hielo y polvo.*

Saturn with 6 of its moons (not to scale)
Saturno con 6 de sus lunas (no muestra escala actual)

Saturn has many moons. Some of these moons are very big. **Saturn's** largest moon is called Titan.

*Saturno tiene muchas lunas. Algunas de estas son muy grandes. La luna más grande de **Saturno** se llama Titán.*

Uranus and **Neptune** have similar atmospheres composed primarily of hydrogen and helium gases. However, Uranus is unique because of how it is tilted on its axis. It lies almost on its side in relation to the Sun. When the sun rises at its north pole, it stays up for 42 Earth years before it sets!

*Urano y **Neptuno** tienen atmósferas similares, compuestas principalmente por los gases hidrógeno y helio. Sin embargo, Urano es único por la inclinación de su eje. Está casi acostado hacia un lado con respecto al Sol. En su polo norte, entre la salida y la puesta del sol, ¡pasan 42 años terrestres!*

Dark spot
Mancha
oscura

Neptune has a set of rings around it. The rings are very hard to see. **Neptune** might even have a deep ocean. The dark spot on **Neptune** is a great storm.

*Neptuno tiene un grupo de anillos a su alrededor. No es fácil ver los anillos. Es posible que **Neptuno** tenga un océano profundo. La mancha oscura de **Neptuno** es una gran tormenta.*

Pluto was once considered a planet. However, the discoveries of other natural objects in our solar system, just as large as **Pluto**, have caused **astronomers** to reconsider what the term "planet" should mean.

After much debate, many **astronomers** agreed that **Pluto** and some other large, round space objects belonged in a new category named "**dwarf planets**."

*Se creía que **Plutón** era un planeta. Sin embargo, el descubrimiento de otros cuerpos celestes en nuestro sistema solar, tan grandes como **Plutón**, hizo que los **astrónomos** evaluaran lo que significa ser un "planeta".*

*Luego de un gran debate, muchos **astrónomos** acordaron que **Plutón** y otros cuerpos celestes redondos y grandes pertenecen a una nueva categoría llamada "**planetas enanos**".*

Astronomers found a big **dwarf planet**. It is much bigger than **Pluto**. There may be lots of other big **dwarf planets** out in our solar system.

*Los **astrónomos** encontraron un gran **planeta enano**. Es mucho más grande que **Plutón**. Pueden haber muchos otros **planetas enanos** en nuestro sistema solar.*

Earth is our home planet. It's the third planet from the Sun and is the only planet in our solar system that has flowing water on its surface.

About seventy percent of the **Earth's** surface is covered with water. Mountains, volcanoes, valleys, plains, and **deserts** cover the remaining thirty percent.

*La **Tierra** es el planeta donde vivimos. Es el tercer planeta desde el Sol y es el único planeta en nuestro sistema solar por cuya superficie corre agua.*

*Alrededor del setenta por ciento de la superficie de la **Tierra** está cubierto por agua. Las montañas, los volcanes, los valles, las llanuras y los **desiertos** cubren el treinta por ciento restante.*

Earth has one Moon. Our Moon is like a very dry **desert**.

*La **Tierra** tiene una luna. Nuestra Luna es como un **desierto** muy seco.*

23

The Moon has had visitors! It is the only place in our solar system where humans have gone. In 1969, the Apollo 11 spaceship carried astronauts Neil Armstrong and Edwin "Buzz" Aldrin to the Moon to explore its surface. Neil Armstrong was the first person to walk on the Moon.

¡La Luna ha tenido visitantes! Es el único lugar en nuestro sistema solar donde los humanos han llegado. En 1969, la nave espacial Apollo 11 llevó a los astronautas Neil Armstrong y Edwin "Buzz" Aldrin a la Luna para explorar su superficie. Neil Armstrong fue la primera persona que caminó en la Luna.

He left his footprints. There is no air to blow them away. His footprints are still on the Moon.

Él dejó sus huellas. Como no hay aire, no se borran. Sus huellas todavía están en la Luna.

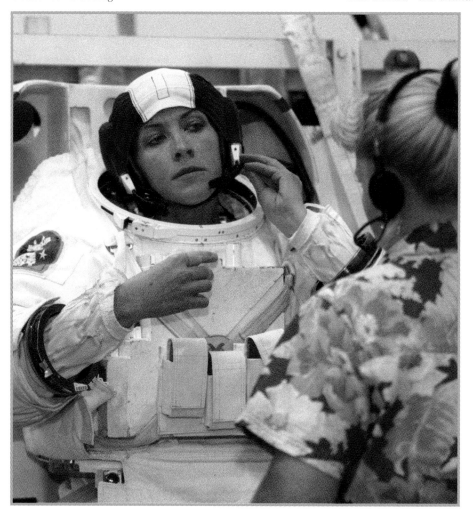

Astronauts go through years of specialized training. They must have strong skills in science, math, and technology.

The **astronauts** that go into space must learn how to function in weightless environments and even learn how to do a space walk.

*Los **astronautas** pasan años de entrenamiento especializado. Deben destacarse en ciencias, matemáticas y tecnología.*

*Los **astronautas** que van al espacio deben aprender cómo trabajar en ambientes sin gravedad y cómo caminar en el espacio.*

Sometimes **astronauts** train underwater. The water helps them know what it might feel like to float in space.

*A veces los **astronautas** se entrenan bajo el agua. El agua les permite saber cómo se siente flotar en el espacio.*

Astronauts must have special **clothing**, food, and equipment to go into space.

During launch and re-entry they wear a special suit that has a helmet, gloves, and boots to protect them from changes in pressure when they leave and return from space.

*Los astronautas deben usar **ropa**, comida y equipo especial para ir al espacio.*

Durante el lanzamiento y el regreso, ellos usan un traje especial que tiene un casco, guantes y botas para protegerlos de los cambios de presión cuando salen y regresan del espacio.

Once they are in space, they can wear the same kind of **clothing** they might wear at home.

*Cuando están en el espacio, pueden usar el mismo tipo de **ropa** que usan en su casa.*

To make it easier to carry food into space, some of the food is freeze-dried—a special process used to remove all of the water from the food. Before astronauts eat their freeze-dried food, they put the water back in it.

Just like many kids, astronauts drink from boxes or pouches, using a straw. With everything floating, drinking from a glass could get very messy!

Para transportar más fácilmente los alimentos al espacio, algunos de estos se congelan y desecan —un proceso especial por el cual se le quita toda el agua a los alimentos. Antes de comerse sus alimentos desecados, los astronautas le ponen agua.

Como muchos niños, los astronautas beben de cajas o bolsas usando una pajilla. ¡Con todo flotando, beber de un vaso podría causar un reguero!

Astronauts eating a meal in space   Los astronautas disfrutan una comida en el espacio

Astronauts like to eat many different kinds of food. Some astronauts like to eat hot dogs. Some like to eat ice cream and cake!

A los astronautas les gusta comer muchos tipos diferentes de alimentos. A algunos astronautas les gustan los perros calientes. ¡A algunos les gusta el helado y el pastel!

Some astronauts learned how to pilot the **Space Shuttle**. The **Space Shuttle** is like an airplane, a rocket, and a spaceship all in one! It takes off like a rocket, circles the Earth like a spaceship, and lands like an airplane.

*Algunos astronautas aprendieron a pilotar el **transbordador espacial**. ¡**El transbordador espacial** es un avión, un cohete y una nave espacial todo en uno! Despega como un cohete, gira alrededor de la Tierra como una nave espacial y aterriza como un avión.*

Astronauts work and sleep on the **Space Shuttle**. Sometimes they sleep in sleeping bags. They are tied to the wall so they won't float away.

Los astronautas trabajan y duermen en el **transbordador espacial**. *A veces ellos duermen en bolsas de dormir. Estas se atan a la pared para que no se vayan flotando.*

A special spacesuit is needed when astronauts leave their spaceship while in orbit. The spacesuit is called an "extravehicular mobility unit", or EMU.

The EMU controls and monitors the astronaut's body temperature and breathing. It has a headphone and microphone so the astronaut can communicate with the Shuttle.

Los astronautas necesitan un traje espacial especial cuando salen de la nave espacial mientras están en órbita. Este traje espacial se llama "Unidad de movilidad extravehicular", o EMU (por sus siglas en inglés).

El EMU controla y monitoriza la temperatura corporal y la respiración del astronauta. Tiene un auricular y un micrófono para que el astronauta pueda comunicarse con el transbordador.

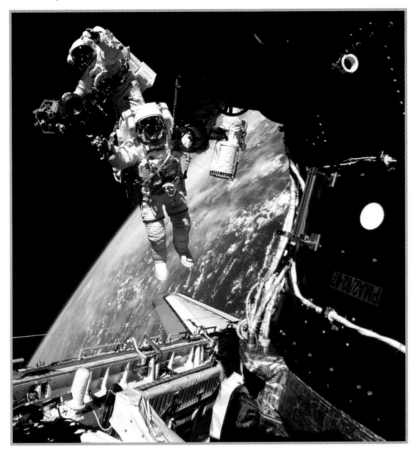

Astronauts may also leave the ship wearing a special backpack. This backpack lets them move freely through space.

Los astronautas también pueden salir de la nave con una mochila especial. Esta mochila les permite moverse libremente a través del espacio.

How would you like to live in space? Some astronauts do. There are teams of astronauts that take turns living and working on **space stations**.

Space stations are enormous satellites that orbit the Earth.

*¿Te gustaría vivir en el espacio? A algunos astronautas les gusta. Hay equipos de astronautas que toman turnos para vivir y trabajar en las **estaciones espaciales**.*

*Las **estaciones espaciales** son satélites enormes que giran alrededor de la Tierra.*

Astronaut on a spacewalk, working on the International Space Station
Astronauta en una caminata espacial, trabajando en la Estación Espacial Internacional

Space stations are made up of many different parts. Astronauts put these parts together in space.

*Las **estaciones espaciales** tienen muchas partes diferentes. Los astronautas conectan estas partes en el espacio.*

International Space Station (Earth and space in the background)
Estación Espacial Internacional (en el fondo, la Tierra y el espacio)

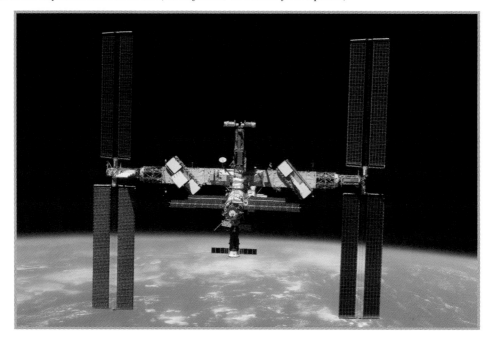

There have been two famous space stations in the past: the United States Skylab, and the Russian Mir.

The biggest space station ever is the International Space Station.

Hubo dos estaciones espaciales famosas en el pasado: Skylab, de los Estados Unidos, y Mir, de Rusia.

La estación espacial más grande de la historia es la Estación Espacial Internacional.

Astronauts working on construction of the International Space Station (Earth in background)
Astronautas trabajando en la construcción de la Estación Espacial Internacional (en el fondo, la Tierra)

Astronauts from many different places live on this space station. They work together to learn more about space.

Astronautas de muchos lugares diferentes viven en esta estación espacial. Ellos trabajan juntos para aprender más acerca del espacio.

There is so much more **interesting** information to learn about space. Maybe someday you will be a scientist or an astronomer. Perhaps you will make new discoveries and explore distant galaxies.

*Hay mucha más información **interesante** por aprender acerca del espacio. Tal vez algún día serás un científico o un astrónomo. Quizás harás nuevos descubrimientos y explorarás galaxias lejanas.*

Illustration of walk on Mars (artist's concept)
Ilustración de una caminata en Marte (creación artística)

What if you were an astronaut? Think of all the **interesting** things you could do. Maybe you could fly to Mars and help build a space station there!

*¿Y si fueras un astronauta? Piensa en todas las cosas **interesantes** que podrías hacer. ¡Tal vez podrías volar a Marte y ayudar a construir una estación espacial allí!*

If you liked **About Space**, here is another
We Both Read® book you are sure to enjoy!

*Si te gustó leer **Acerca del espacio**, ¡seguramente disfrutarás
de leer este otro libro de la serie We Both Read®!*

Featuring beautiful illustrations and written with
the assistance of dinosaur specialist Dr. Matthew
Lamanna, this book explores the lives of many
species of these ancient creatures.

*Destacando bellas ilustraciones y escrito con
la ayuda de un especialista en dinosaurios, el
Dr. Matthew Lamanna, este libro explora la vida de
muchas de las especies de estas criaturas antiguas.*

To see all the *We Both Read®* books that are available,
just go online to **www.TreasureBayBooks.com**

*Para ver todos los libros disponibles de la serie We Both Read®,
visita nuestra página web: www.TreasureBayBooks.com*